A is for Abraham

A Jewish Family Alphabet

Written by Richard Michelson and Illustrated by Ron Mazellan

I offer with my admiration,
Respect and love, this dedication:
I count my blessings every day
That Jennifer's my letter J.

RICHARD

✎

for Chris

RON

The author and publisher wish to acknowledge the following people for their
gracious consultation: Natalie Blitt, Rabbi Justin David, Judy Gitenstein,
Becka McKay, Jennifer Michelson, Rabbi S. Robert Morais, Lisa Perlbinder,
Lisa Silverman, and Marcie Simons.

Sleeping Bear Press

310 North Main Street, Suite 300
Chelsea, MI 48118
www.sleepingbearpress.com

© 2008 Sleeping Bear Press is an imprint of Gale, a part of Cengage Learning.

Printed and bound in the United States.

10 9 8 7 6 5 4 3 2

Library of Congress Cataloging-in-Publication Data

Michelson, Richard.
A is for abraham : a Jewish family alphabet / written by Richard Michelson;
Illustrated by Ron Mazellan.
p. cm.
Summary: "This illustrated alphabet book is for a general audience covering
many important people, rituals, and traditions such as Bar and Bat Mitzvah,
King David, Israel, Klezmer Music, Passover, Tikkun Olam, and many more.
Text from A to Z includes simple poetry for younger readers and detailed
expository text for older readers"—Provided by publisher.
ISBN 978-1-58536-322-3
1. Judaism. I. Mazellan, Ron. II. Title.
BM45.M53 2008
296.03--dc22   2008012615

Author's Note

This alphabet book is intended for a general audience. Jewish customs and beliefs often vary by denomination and locale, and I could never hope to satisfy all readers. If your ritual or tradition differs from that described in this book, think of it as an opportunity to share and explain.

Whether you are Reform, Conservative, Orthodox, unaffiliated, or part of the more recent Reconstructionist, Renewal, or Humanistic movements, I hope these pages will help begin a family discussion. Judaism is a tree with many different branches, but all are nourished by the same roots, and we need to support and respect each other. It is my belief that:

**Like a choir sounds best when it blends different voices,
Jews should applaud Jews who've made different choices.**

A is for Abraham, father of Jews
(father of Muslims, and all Christians, too).

His wife's name was Sarah, and when angels blessed her,
she too became our common ancestor.

Four thousand years ago, people worshipped idols and believed in many gods, but Abraham believed that there was only one God. Abraham, his son Isaac, and Isaac's son Jacob are known as the three patriarchs (fathers) of the Jewish people. Sarah (Abraham's wife), Rebecca (Isaac's wife), and Leah and Rachel (Jacob's wives) are the four matriarchs (mothers).

Abraham's name means "father of many," and Abraham was indeed the spiritual father of many people. Muslims are descendents of Abraham's first son, Ishmael, whose mother was Hagar. Jews and Christians are descendants of Abraham's second son, Isaac, whose mother was Sarah. The name Sarah means "princess." Sarah lived to be 127, and Abraham was 175 years old when he died.

Even though Abraham and Sarah lived almost four thousand years ago, today in America, Abraham and Sarah remain popular names.

A a

Bb

B's for our Bar and Bat Mitzvahs because
it's fun to grow older and learn Jewish laws.
When we turn thirteen it's the rabbi's opinion
that you can't call us babies. We count towards a minyan!

Bar Mitzvah means "son of the commandments" and *Bat Mitzvah* means "daughter of the commandments." When a Jewish boy turns thirteen, he becomes a Bar Mitzvah. Girls become a Bat Mitzvah at age twelve, although many choose to celebrate at thirteen. The service (when the boy or girl is "called to the Torah," and has the honor of reciting a blessing) is the public acknowledgment of the child's "coming of age." Until then it is the parents' job to encourage their child to observe the *mitzvot* (the Jewish commandments). At thirteen, children become responsible for their own actions, and they count towards a *minyan*, which is the number of people needed to conduct certain prayer services (although until recently girls were not counted, nor were they allowed to lead services). Having at least ten adults helps to encourage a sense of community among Jews.

The term *mitzvah* is often used to mean any act of kindness, and Jewish children are urged to perform a mitzvah, like helping to feed the hungry, as part of their bar or bat mitzvah preparation.

Most Jewish celebrations have traditional foods associated with them. Challah, for instance, is a braided loaf of bread eaten to celebrate the arrival of the Sabbath. Generations of Jewish mothers and grandmothers (bubbes) have given their children chicken soup to cure all kinds of sicknesses. Chickens are nutritious and were often the only meat that poor Eastern European Jews could afford. In America many "Jewish foods" like bagels and lox and knishes are popular, even among non-Jews.

Observant Jews follow strict rules about what foods (and food combinations) they are permitted to eat. If these foods are properly prepared, they are called "kosher." Even chocolate must meet strict standards during its preparation. During Chanukah, Jews often give their children chocolate coins. No one knows how this custom started, but some parents hide chocolates in the pages of prayer books to encourage their children to study, and to teach them that "learning is sweet."

The Hebrew word *chai* means "life." It is made of the two Hebrew letters *chet* and *yod*, and highlights Judaism's focus on the importance of everyone's life. Before beginning a festive meal, the typical Jewish toast is *l'chayim*, meaning "to life."

C c

C could be the challah that my bubbe used to braid,
or C could be the chicken soup, when I was sick, she made,
or chocolate coins on Chanukah we added to our coffers.
But I say C should be for *chai*, to "life" and all it offers.

King David is one of the greatest figures in the Bible and Jewish history. As a young shepherd he slew the giant Goliath and saved his people. He became king and united the many scattered Jewish tribes into a strong nation. He planned the First Temple, which was built by his son, Solomon. David played the lyre, a stringed instrument similar to a harp. According to tradition, David also wrote the Psalms, which includes some of the greatest Hebrew love poems to God.

Jews have long had a love of music and poetry, which continues to the present day. Jewish musicians and composers like Bob Dylan, Leonard Bernstein, George Gershwin, and Richard Rogers have had a great influence on contemporary American music. Some of the most influential American poets are also Jewish—among them are Allen Ginsberg, Adrienne Rich, and Stanley Kunitz.

D is for the shepherd David, who according to tradition
was great as King,
but greater still,
as poet and musician.

America is a country made up of immigrants. Many Jews began to come to America from Eastern Europe in the late 1800s, and they continued to come in great waves until the mid 1900s, hoping for religious freedom and a better life. Ellis Island, near Liberty Island where the Statue of Liberty stands, was where most ships docked. A famous poem, written by the American Jewish poet Emma Lazarus, is engraved on the base of the Statue. It includes these words:

> "Give me your tired, your poor,
> Your huddled masses yearning to
>   breathe free,
> The wretched refuse of your
>   teeming shore.
> Send these, the homeless,
>   tempest-tost to me,
> I lift my lamp beside the golden door!"

Albert Einstein was one of the Jews who came to America through Ellis Island. He was one of the greatest scientists in history, and his name is often used to describe anyone who is a genius ("she's a real Einstein!"). Einstein was a sloppy dresser and his wild hair was usually uncombed. And even though he became a brilliant scientist, he was not a good student in school. Einstein said that "Imagination is more important than knowledge."

E e

E is for Ellis Island near Miss Liberty's new home
where she welcomes all the immigrants, and reads them Emma's poem.

And E's for Einstein's fine idea: E equals MC squared—
which proves that even geniuses forget to comb their hair.

F is for Five Scrolls and the five books of the Torah,
which we study with the Talmud (that's the Mishna and Gemara).
Each time we left our homeland, they're the first things that we took.
And today the Jews are still known as the People of the Book.

The Torah can refer to the first five books of the Bible: Genesis, Exodus, Leviticus, Numbers, and Deuteronomy (also called the Pentateuch); or it can include all the books that Christians know as "the Old Testament," which Jews call the Tanakh; or it can refer to all Jewish teachings. The Torahs used in synagogues are hand written on scrolls.

The Five Scrolls are five short biblical books which are part of the third section of the Tanakh, called the Ketuvim (or Writings). They are often grouped together in Jewish tradition, and each is read on a different Jewish holiday. They include The Song of Songs, The Book of Ruth, Lamentations, Ecclesiastes, and The Book of Esther.

The Talmud is a collection of Jewish teachings that help to interpret the Torah. It is composed of the Mishna, early oral laws that were written down in the second century, and the Gemara, rabbinical commentary written down over the next few centuries.

Jewish law is based on the material found in the Torah. Whenever the Jews were forced out of their homeland by invading armies, they brought their Holy Scrolls with them in exile. Even today American Jews have a strong literary tradition, both Biblical and secular. Many of the most important American writers in recent times have been Jewish, including Philip Roth, Bernard Malamud, Grace Paley, and Saul Bellow.

A golem is like a Frankenstein monster made out of mud and clay that, according to Jewish legend, can be brought to life and made to follow its master's orders by reciting a secret Hebrew prayer or by writing special words on its forehead. The most famous golem was created by Rabbi Judah Loew of Prague over 500 years ago. The golem was supposed to protect the Jews from attacks by their neighbors. Some people say that this golem is still hidden in a coffin in the attic of the Old Synagogue in Prague, where it can be brought back to life if it is needed.

Many plays and stories have been written about the golem, and other superhuman figures. Even the comic book hero Superman was written by two American Jews named Siegel and Schuster, who based their story on the Golem of Prague. More recently the golem has appeared in *The Simpsons* television show; in picture books by Isaac Bashevis Singer and others; and in Michael Chabon's Pulitzer prize-winning novel, *The Amazing Adventures of Kavalier and Clay.*

G is one gigantic Golem.
I hope he's on our side!
Can Rabbi Loew control him?
In case he can't, let's hide!

G g

H h

Hebrew starts with Alef, Bet. The **H** is pronounced: Hay.
It's read backwards from right to left. We read it when we pray.
Israelis read and write in Hebrew every single day.
And they say *we* read backwards. I guess both ways are okay.

Hebrew is an ancient language that was spoken by most Jews in Biblical times. It is written and read from right to left and the alphabet has 22 letters that look very different from English letters. Most American Jews still recite their prayers in Hebrew, but almost two thousand years ago, when the Jews were forced to leave their homeland after the destruction of the Second Temple, they became visitors in other lands and two other major Jewish languages evolved.

Yiddish, a mixture of German, Polish, and Hebrew, was the everyday language spoken by three-quarters of the world's Jews for over one thousand years. These Jews are known as Ashkenazi Jews and their descendants make up approximately 80 percent of the world's Jews. Ladino is spoken by Sephardic Jews, who primarily come from Spanish speaking countries. They were forced to leave Spain during the Spanish Inquisition. Many of these Jews moved to Portugal, Greece, North Africa, and the Balkans. When they were forced to leave these countries, most moved to the southwestern United States, Mexico, and South America.

בני חורין ושוויס בער

מצפוך, לפיכך חובה

אתוה

In 1948 when the country of Israel was established, Hebrew was chosen to be the official language. Eliezer Ben-Yehuda helped revive the language and he is known as the "Father of Modern Hebrew." Because in their daily lives most Jews had been speaking Yiddish, Ladino, or the language of the country where they were living, Hebrew hadn't developed many modern expressions and Ben-Yehuda had to make up hundreds of Hebrew words, including those for treats such as ice cream or jelly.

The Hebrew text in the artwork is from Article 1 of the Universal Declaration of Human Rights:

> "All human beings are born free and equal in dignity and rights. They are endowed with reason and conscience and should act towards one another in a spirit of brotherhood."

I i

I is for Israel. Our people used to roam
from land to land as strangers. We had no place called home.
But now all Jews are welcome in the land of milk and honey—
black or white, boy or girl, rich or without money.

Abraham's grandson Jacob was also called Israel and all the Jewish people living today are descended from one of Jacob's twelve sons who were known as "the children of Israel." The land where they settled became the Jewish homeland. For over 3,000 years, Jews have regarded the Land of Israel as both a Holy Land and as a Promised Land. It is called a land of milk and honey in the Bible, because it is thought of as a place of comfort and sweetness and abundance.

Starting around 1250 BCE, a series of Jewish kingdoms and states existed in the region for more than a thousand years. The Jews were forced off their land in the year 70 CE when the Second Temple was destroyed and they were defeated by the Romans. It wasn't until the country of Israel was established on May 14, 1948, following a vote by the United Nations, that the Jews regained their homeland.

Israel is a tiny country located in the Middle East. It is about the size of the American state of New Jersey. While many Jews live outside of Israel, and many non-Jews live in Israel, all Jews may automatically become Israeli citizens if they choose to be.

"Next year in Jerusalem," is what my parents say.
    That's why I choose Jerusalem to be my letter J.
"The Jewel of the Holy Land!" It sure would be a pity
    if I never got to see the world's most Golden City.

Jerusalem is the holiest city in Judaism. It was King David's capital and the site of King Solomon's Temple (Solomon was David's son) and the Second Temple. King Solomon's Temple was destroyed by the Babylonian army in 586 BCE, and the Jews were forced to leave their homeland. Ever since, many Jews have lived in the Diaspora (the settlements of Jews outside of their homeland). Some of these Jews long to return to the Land of Israel and it is a tradition to face Jerusalem during prayer.

Jerusalem is also a Holy City for Christians and Muslims. It is where Jesus died and where Muhammad began his journey to heaven. It is one of the most beautiful cities in the world, and all buildings in Jerusalem must include stones quarried from near the city. These stones tend to be of a gold or reddish hue, and when the sun is setting, it makes the whole city look like it is made of gold.

J j

K is for Klezmer music with its clarinets and fiddle.
My head grooves,
   then my feet move.
      Soon
      I'm rotating
         my middle.

K k

You can't sit still when you listen to klezmer music. It is a style of music in Yiddish culture normally characterized by wailing, squealing sounds of clarinets, along with a fiddle and a flute or accordion. Klezmer music is often played at Jewish weddings and other joyful celebrations, so the melodies are lively and the tempos fast. It is most similar to Dixieland or jazz music, and klezmer has recently become very popular, even among non-Jews in the United States.

At a traditional Jewish wedding, dancing to help entertain the bride and groom is considered a mitzvah. Guests also take turns dancing in the center of a circle and then they lift the recently married couple on chairs and parade them around the room while the klezmer musicians play faster and faster, and everyone claps and has a good time.

L is for this Lulav branch, around which I have braided
two willow and three myrtle twigs. All by myself I made it.
My left hand holds my etrog. All the colors are so pretty.
and through our sukkah ceiling I see stars light up the city.

Sukkot is a joyful autumn festival that celebrates the harvest. It is a time to give thanks and to count our blessings. Special prayers are said while holding four different types of plants. The lulav is a long palm branch that is held with two willow and three myrtle twigs. The etrog is a fourth plant that looks like a lemon. The lulav and etrog are waved up and down, and right and left, and to all the corners of the world and heaven and Earth to symbolize that God is everywhere.

For Sukkot, some Jews make a small temporary house called a *sukkah*. It is like building a fort in your backyard. It reminds us of the tents in which the Jewish people lived during forty years of wandering in the desert. Children decorate the sukkah, and branches can be used to make a roof through which you can see the stars and the sky.

It is a mitzvah to invite friends, neighbors, and even strangers who do not have a sukkah of their own. Jewish hospitality has a long tradition going back to Abraham, who would sit outside of his desert tent and invite travelers to share a meal.

Ll

M m

M is for Mattathias Maccabee and his son, Judah the Lion,
who mended the Menorah when he recaptured Mt. Zion.
Miracle of miracles, it burned for eight long nights
which is why today we celebrate the Festival of Lights.

When Alexander the Great ruled most of the Middle East, he allowed the Jews to continue to practice their own religion as long as they followed his laws. When King Antiochus IV came to power, he ruled that the Jews could no longer practice their own religion, but instead, under penalty of death, must follow the Greek way of worship. Most Jews did so, and lived peacefully under Syrian rule.

But Mattathias, a Jew living in the mountains of Modin, refused, and in 165 BCE, he and his five sons led a revolt against the Syrian army. It was the first war ever fought, not for land or wealth, but for religious freedom. If the Jews had not triumphed there would be no Judaism or Christianity today.

After Mattathias' death, Judah Maccabee took command of the Jewish forces, and recaptured the Temple where he found the golden menorah broken. Although there was only enough oil to light the menorah for one night, it burned for eight days. Jews have been celebrating Chanukah, or "rededication," ever since. While Chanukah was traditionally a minor holiday, in America where it usually falls in December, its proximity to Christmas has made it one of the most celebrated of the holidays.

Noah and the Ark is many children's favorite Bible story. God instructed Noah to build an enormous ark, which was more than 500 feet (150 meters) long, and to board two of every animal in existence. When it rained for forty days and forty nights, these animals were saved from drowning. When the rain finally stopped and the waters receded, Noah, his family, and the animals left the Ark and re-created the world. Since that time, after every rain, God sends a rainbow as a promise that such a flood will never happen again.

Judaism stresses that we should always treat animals with kindness. Eating meat is permitted, but causing unnecessary suffering is forbidden, and an animal's life must be taken in a way that causes them the least amount of pain. Many of the greatest Biblical figures were shepherds who cared for their flock, rather than hunters, as in many other cultures. Killing animals for sport is not allowed. Animals are even allowed to rest on the Sabbath, so don't ask your dog to bring you the Saturday morning newspaper.

Two by two the animals
ascended up the plank.
When all were through,
the hippos knew
who it was they should thank.
A roar resounded round the ark,
both upper deck and lower.

Hip, Hip, Hooray! You've saved the day.
Let's hear three cheers
for Noah!

O o

Oneg Shabbat literally means "delight of the Sabbath." The Sabbath, or Shabbat, as it is known in Hebrew, is a special day of rest and joy, when we can forget about all of our everyday concerns and devote ourselves to family, study, and new beginnings.

Shabbat is the most important of all Jewish observances, and it is the only holiday listed in the Ten Commandments. In America many people are used to "taking the weekend off," but in ancient times the idea of a day of rest was revolutionary. Only the very wealthy could afford a day of rest. The Bible says that God rested on the seventh day after making the world, and Shabbat is a day set aside for us to remember our freedom.

An Oneg Shabbat is a gathering of Jews in a synagogue or private home to express their happiness that the Sabbath has arrived. There is often music, games, good food, and conversation. Shabbat begins at sunset on each Friday night when candles are lit and a blessing is recited. Challah and wine (or grape juice) receive a special blessing at the beginning of the meal.

On each Friday night I am filled with delight
at the Oneg Shabbat's first flicker of light.
Sunday through Thursday is fine but the best
day of the week is the one day we rest.

P What's number one on my holiday rater?
assover wins each year. I love the Seder.
There's kugel and karpas and I eat a lotta
    matzo balls after we read the Haggadah.

(Purim's my favorite holiday too,
    so please turn the page to the next letter—Q).

Of all the Jewish holidays, Passover is one of the most commonly observed, even by otherwise non-observant Jews. It is the time when Jewish families often get together to share a special meal, called a Seder. The *afikoman*, a piece of matzo, is hidden at the start of the meal, after which the children look for it, and the finder gets a prize for its safe return to the table. Visit a typical Jewish Ashkenazi home at Passover and you'll likely find gefilte fish, matzo-ball soup, horseradish, or potato kugel, all known as "traditional" Jewish foods. Visit a Sephardic home, however, and the menu most likely would include dishes such as roasted lamb, tabouli salad, and cooked spiced vegetables.

The text of the Passover Seder is written in a book called the Haggadah. The Haggadah explains some of the practices and symbols of the holiday, and it tells the story of how the Jews were slaves in Egypt and how they were led to freedom. During the Seder the youngest child present asks the question: "Why is this night different from all other nights?" The answer is the story of Passover.

P p

Purim is one of the most joyful and fun holidays on the Jewish calendar. It is customary to hold carnival-like celebrations on Purim, which is known as the Jewish Mardi Gras. Many schools put on plays, which retell the story of the holiday, and the children boo, hiss, stamp their feet, and rattle noisemakers whenever the name of Haman is mentioned during the play.

The King of Persia had fallen in love with the beautiful Esther, not knowing that she was Jewish. The King's advisor, Haman, convinced the King to kill all the Jewish people in the Kingdom, because Esther's Uncle Mordechai would not bow down to him. It took great courage for Esther to reveal her religion and tell the King about Haman's plot, but she saved the Jewish people, and Haman was hanged on the gallows.

Many Jews love to eat hamantaschen during the Purim carnival. These triangular fruit-filled cookies represent Haman's three-cornered hat.

Q
q

Q's for Queen Esther. Guess who I played
        in the synagogue's Purim parade masquerade?
We laughed,
      stomped,
      and hollered,
            but the best part was noshin'
those Haman hats filled with fruit called hamantaschen.

R r

R is for Rabbi, our spiritual leader,
part scholar, part counselor, and part Torah reader.

Although they both wrote in the Medieval Ages,
Rashi and Rambam are remembered as sages.

A rabbi is a Jewish religious teacher who serves as the spiritual and legal guide of their congregation and community. Two of the greatest rabbis of all time were Rashi and Rambam.

Rambam is also known as Maimonides, or Rabbi Moses ben Maimon. A Sephardic Jew, he was born in Spain in 1135. Besides being a rabbi, he was also a physician, scientist, and philosopher. He wrote an important book of Jewish philosophy called *The Guide for the Perplexed*. Rashi is also known as Rabbi Solomon ben Isaac. He was born in France in 1040, and although he worked as a grower of grapes, he wrote one of the most important commentaries on the Bible and almost every edition of the Talmud now includes Rashi's opinions.

Not all rabbi names begin with the letter R. Hillel was one of the greatest rabbis. He lived more than two thousand years ago and was known for his kindness to all people. When a non-Jew challenged him to describe Judaism in the amount of time that he could stand on one foot, Hillel answered by telling him, "That which is hateful to you, do not do to your neighbor. That is the whole Torah; the rest is commentary. Go and study it." In America we call this "The Golden Rule."

The *Sh'ma* is considered by many to be the most important prayer in Judaism. It says you should *Love the Lord your God with all your heart and all your mind and all your strength.* These words are also written on a tiny piece of paper and put inside the *mezuzah,* which is a small case nailed to the right front doorpost of many Jewish homes. Parents are told to *Never forget these commands and teach them to your children* so the Sh'ma is usually the first prayer that Jewish children learn. It is recited at bedtime to help protect you from nighttime fears. Many Jews also recite it in the morning, and before reading the Torah, and at the end of Yom Kippur.

A good way to say the Sh'ma is to close and cover your eyes with your right hand to help you concentrate, and then to recite it out loud:

Hear, O Israel: the Lord our God, the Lord is One.

Sh'ma Yis-ra-eil, A-do-nai E-lo-hei-nu, A-do-nai E-chad.

S

S

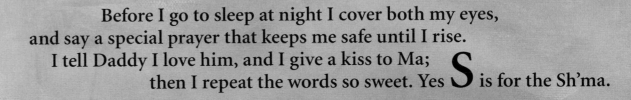

Before I go to sleep at night I cover both my eyes,
and say a special prayer that keeps me safe until I rise.
I tell Daddy I love him, and I give a kiss to Ma;
then I repeat the words so sweet. Yes S is for the Sh'ma.

T is for Tikkun Olam. There is just no getting 'round it:
We each should leave the world a little better than we found it.

Tikkun olam is a Hebrew term that means "repairing the world." The Jewish tradition encourages everyone to help those less fortunate than themselves. The term was first used in the Mishna, where it encouraged extra protection for the disadvantaged and argued for the freeing of slaves. Many Jews today interpret this to mean they should help all oppressed people, always try to act with kindness, and give *tzedakah* (charity) to those in need. Judaism does not view these as generous acts for which we are to be congratulated, but simply as behaving as we should.

Tikkun olam is also often interpreted to mean that we also have a responsibility to try and improve our earthly surroundings and make the planet better for both ourselves and future generations.

There are between 12 and 15 million Jews in the world today, according to most estimates. Approximately 6 million Jews live in the United States of America where they make up less than 2 percent of the population. An additional 5 to 6 million Jews live in Israel. Worldwide, Jews account for less than one quarter of 1 percent of the population.

Although the United States, founded by those seeking religious and economic freedoms, has been more welcoming to Jews than most countries have been throughout history, anti-Semitism still exists even here, and all Jews must continue to fight for their freedoms, as well as those of all minorities.

During the Holocaust, Jews throughout Europe were required to sew a yellow cloth Star of David (a six pointed Jewish star) on their shirts and jackets as a badge of shame. Today many American Jews wear jewelry with a Star of David as a badge of pride.

U u

U is for the country called U. S. of A.
where half the world's Jews are living today,
and where we are free to worship as we choose.
We're proud to say loudly that YES we are Jews.

Vv

Jewish visual arts do not have as long a tradition as Jewish music and literature, perhaps because many Jews considered the Ten Commandments' prohibition against making graven images to mean that they could not draw pictures of people, since people are made "in God's image." In the twentieth century, however, many Jews became prominent in the European Modern Art movements. Perhaps the best known is Marc Chagall who was born in the Russian village of Vitebsk. In many of his paintings, Chagall liked to remember his poor but happy Jewish childhood. He used bright colors, and he loved to put farm and circus animals in his pictures.

Recently many American Jewish artists have used Jewish themes in their artwork, including Leonard Baskin, Ben Shahn, Judy Chicago, and Maurice Sendak who wrote the children's book classic *Where The Wild Things Are*.

And **V** is for vaudeville's borscht belt: Magic tricks, and quick-witted comics performing their shticks.

V is also for vaudeville, a type of variety show, which often included song-and-dance routines, juggling, magic, and comedy. This was very popular in the upstate New York Catskill Mountains (known as the borscht belt), where resorts catered to Jews at a time when most hotels had signs that said "no Jews or Negroes." Among the many Jewish comedians who got their start at these hotels were Mel Brooks, Phyllis Diller, Jerry Lewis, the Marx Brothers, and the Three Stooges. They redefined American humor and influenced the most recent generation of American comics, like Jerry Seinfeld, Roseanne Barr, and Jon Stewart. Jewish humor is what many people think of as American humor.

V is for Vitebsk where young Chagall first drew
his village of dreams filled with horses hued blue,
and where green violinists would fiddle their praise
for the violet-eyed brides flying by with bouquets.

King David designed a great Jewish Temple to glorify God, and his son Solomon built it. The holiest place in the Temple, known as the Holiest of Holies, was a room in which the two tablets of the Ten Commandments were kept. After 400 years the Babylonians destroyed the Temple, but it was rebuilt on the same site. That Temple was destroyed by the Romans in the year 70 CE. Only the Western Wall, one of the four walls which surrounded and guarded the Temple Mount, remained standing, and it is still standing tall after more than two thousand years.

Jews and many other people from all over the world come here to pray, and they often write down their prayers and leave the papers in tiny cracks in the walls. Men and women pray at different sections of the wall. The Western Wall used to be known as the Wailing Wall since so many Jews came here to express their sadness at the destruction of the Temple, and the loss of their home- land for almost two thousand years. Today the Western Wall is a popular spot for many American children to celebrate their bar or bat mitzvahs.

W
W

W is for the Western Wall,
which for two thousand years,
has stood up tall and welcomed all
to share their tears and prayers.

X is for eXodus. Yes. I can tell
it starts with an "e" (I know how to spell).
But with two letters left I'd not mentioned Moses
and thought that I'd better before this book closes.

Moses was the greatest prophet, leader, and teacher that Judaism has ever known. Moses led the Jews out of Egyptian slavery, and across the Red Sea to freedom. He led them through the desert, where they wandered for forty years. He received the Ten Commandments and the Torah on Mount Sinai and delivered God's laws to his people. He then led them to the Promised Land.

This story is told in the Biblical book of Exodus, and it is repeated each year at the Passover Seder. There have been many American films about Moses, including *The Ten Commandments*, and the story of Moses movie, *The Prince of Egypt*. During the time of slavery in America, many African Americans celebrated the story of Moses leading the Jewish people to freedom, and Harriet Tubman, a former slave who helped many slaves escape their bondage, was known as the American Moses.

The Jewish High Holy Days refer to Rosh Hashanah, Yom Kippur, and the ten-day period between them.

Rosh Hashanah is the Jewish New Year. It is a time to look back at the mistakes of the past and plan the changes you will make in the future. Some Jews walk to a body of water and toss breadcrumbs into the river, symbolically casting off the past year's sins. This custom is called *tashlich*. Some families also eat apples dipped in honey to hope for a sweet new year.

The ten days between Rosh Hashanah and Yom Kippur are known as the Days of Awe, when we can apologize, and try to make up for the wrongs we have committed against both God and our friends.

Yom Kippur, the "Day of Atonement," is probably the most important holiday of the Jewish year. Many Jews will fast, attend synagogue, and not go to work or school on this day. It is a good time to think of those without the good fortune to have enough to eat. Because of the fast day, many people think of Yom Kippur as a day of sadness, but it is a holiday of joy and contemplation, and a chance for a fresh start.

Why do we gather breadcrumbs and then toss our sins away?
Why do we wear our yarmulkes to synagogue and pray?
Because our holiest holiday is almost here. That's why!
Yes! Yom Kippur is coming soon. That's why
it is my Y.

Z is for Zayde whose bedtime like mine
is eight o'clock each night (on holidays, nine).
He reads me a story. One more, I beg, please.

But by now he's snoring his loud Zayde
ZZZZZzzzzzzzzzzzzzzzzzzzzzzzzzzzzzzzzzzzzzzzzzzzzzzs.

Zayde is the Yiddish word for Grandpa.
Grandma is called *Bubbe*.

For Jews the home is the center of Jewish
life. Everything central to the practice of
Judaism can be found in the home. A warm,
loving family life has always been central
for the Jews who, over the centuries, have
found safety and trust in the home and in
the community. Holidays are so important
because they bring families together. This
idea of a close and loving family is still
very strong among Jews today.

Zz

The Hebrew Alphabet

ט	ח	ז	ו	ה	ד	ג	ב	א
Tet	Khet	Zayin	Vav	He	Dalet	Gimel	Bet/Vet	Alef
(T)	(Ch)	(Z)	(V/O/U)	(H)	(D)	(G)	(B/V)	(Silent)

ס	ן	נ	ם	מ	ל	ך	כ	י
Samekh	Nun Sofit	Nun	Mem Sofit	Mem	Lamed	Kaf Sofit	Kaf	Yod
(S)	(N)	(N)	(M)	(M)	(L)	(Kh)	(K/Kh)	(Y)

ת	ש	ר	ק	ץ	צ	ף	פ	ע
Tav	Shin	Resh	Kuf	Tsadi Sofit	Tsadi	Pe Sofit	Pe	Ayin
(T)	(Sh/S)	(R)	(K)	(Tz)	(Tz)	(F)	(P/F)	(Silent)